CONTENTS

INTRODUCTION

My name is Susan, and I'm an alcoholic.

I am also an optimist. An undying optimist. My glass is ever half-full, my skies blue, and my head and heart continually open to new and wondrous possibilities.

This little guide is my partial *thank you* to my Higher Power. (Who happens to be the God of my understanding, though I understand very little about God. I only know He's got my back.) My ongoing and ever-present gratitude to God, my family (both by birth and through my recovery program), and my friends far and wide is expressed by me daily. It's through the choices I make (or don't make), chances I take, and joy I feel at having another opportunity to live today to the best of my ability ... with some help, of course.

My hope is one person will come across this little tome and find something in it that inspires him or her to wait five more minutes before using or continue searching for that one little scrap of sunlight that can help make today a day to celebrate. There is a saying that is popular in some twelve-step programs: "Don't give up five minutes before your miracle." If you can hang in there (whether it's five minutes, a few hours, or a few days), it will be worth it. I promise you.

Is it worth it? Oh, is it ever.

Are *you* worth it? Absolutely, and yes, and again: *yes.*

1

THE END. AND THE BEGINNING.

Recovery. Whether you've recently found yourself drinking, using too much, or woke up in a jail cell, you're here now. Good on you. Now get ready for the hardest thing you've ever had to do.

I know this journey is tougher than hell. Recovery is not for the faint of heart. It *is* a struggle; at times, it feels as though it will never be worth it. It would be so much easier to say, "Fuck it!" and pick up again. Remember this little bit of wisdom I carry close to my heart each and every day: before you pour that drink or take that pill, play the tape all the way through. Think of what that *one* will lead to. And what that will lead to. And what that will lead to. Do I need to remind you of the shakes, so terrifically powerful you couldn't bring a cup (or spoon, fork, or straw) to your mouth without spilling the contents everywhere, except where intended?

What about being so sick to your stomach all you can do is dry heave at the sink, vision marred by the endless tears pouring from your eyes, sink stained with the blood you're bringing up? Sitting up in bed because to lie down hurts too much (and the shivers won't allow you to lie down anyway)? How about trying to walk, feeling as if you'll step wrong and fall over your own feet? Trying to speak and having your breath catch in your throat, heart hammering roughly 1,000 beats a minute, surely readying itself to burst out of your chest? Hands shaking so much you can't even write your name? Tossing and turning in your bed, sheets soaked with sweat, yet so cold you feel as if you'll never be warm again?

Remember that time you woke up in the middle of the night, not knowing if it was dark or light, not knowing what day of the week it was, not knowing if you'd ever be able to wake up normal again? (You won't, by the way. You're an addict. There is nothing normal about us except the fact that we're abnormal.) Remember the fear that struck you as cold and hard as a wet towel, right in your face, right in your chest? Remember the worry about what you did, said, didn't say, thought you'd thought but realized you'd said out loud? Remember talking to someone the next day, fishing with generalized questions to see if they'd spill the beans about your latest drunken tirade on your social media outlet of choice? The one you hoped you'd only dreamed about, but you're pretty sure you actually did? Remember heading out to your car (if you could find where you parked it) to see if there were any dents, scratches, or worse? Remember being twelve sheets to the wind, crying, praying, pleading for help?

Do you remember?

If you do, good. Don't ever forget that feeling. Don't ever lose that memory. Keep it close to you, like a lucky penny. You know it's there. You know you can pull it out and touch it if you need to, but most of the time, you don't need to. Knowing it's there is enough.

> BEFORE YOU POUR THAT DRINK OR TAKE THAT PILL, PLAY THE TAPE ALL THE WAY THROUGH.

That's what it means to play the tape through. Everything has a beginning, middle, and end. As a drunk (or if you prefer, an alcoholic, pill popper, junkie, or simply a lost and hurting soul), your beginnings always start out fine, but as soon as you enter any mind-altering substance into the equation, boom! The middle and the end don't play as you'd planned. The kicker is it's not your fault. It's what we're hard-wired to do because we're addicts. It isn't our natural state to be clean and sober, and that's why recovery, especially before all of the blessings start to pour in, is so ridiculously hard.

I can already hear the voices being raised. "She said it's not my fault! Whoopee! That means I can't control it, and I don't have to take any responsibility for it! Shit the bed, let's go get a drink!" Hold up, bud. I *did* say it's not your fault, but that does not give you a hall pass to go back to drinking or using. That would be stoking the fire in a furnace that not only gives off heat but also invisible, deadly fumes.

We *are* hard-wired a different way, and staying clean *does* go against our nature. I think that's why once we get completely involved in a good, strong, solid course of recovery, the good stuff starts to come fast and hard. It's God's way of reminding you what you're doing is tough, and it *is* work, and it does wear you out at times, but man, does it pay off. In more ways than one.

2

PINK CLOUDS OFTEN SIGNIFY STORMS NEARBY

This little book isn't a step-by-step guide to getting sober or clean. It's meant as a source of information, inspiration, and things to be aware of as you're starting your new chapter in life. Though it's written by an optimistic drunk, I'm also a realist. (I am aware it's an odd combo of descriptors, but it's how I've classified myself for as long as I can remember. I am a glass-half-full gal, but I also know I need to check that glass to make sure it doesn't have a crack in it.)

One thing most of us become aware of pretty quickly in recovery is how good it feels to wake up sober without any of the worrisome, nagging thoughts that often accompany any accomplished addict upon waking. Where am I? What did I do last night? How did I get home? What did I say/hear/post? Do I still have a job? Do I have anything left? (On that last one, if you're an alcoholic/addict, you know exactly what I mean. If you're not, we as abusers of all things chemical almost instantly start looking for more once awake. If there's nothing left, the first order of the day is to score more so the shakes/sweats/heaves won't set in. I know, I know. It sounds like a strange way to start your day, and it is for normal people. For people deeply mired in addiction, it's not a *want to*. It's a *need to* so you can avoid becoming terribly, horribly sick.)

After a few twenty-four hours of waking up without being physically sick, many of us start to get it. This is what normal people do. Normal people go to sleep at night and wake up in the morning, ready to go to work, take the kids to school, or head to classes. Simple things like having a cup of coffee or a walk with the dog are incomprehensible to people in the grips of addiction. Coffee won't stay down, and the dog walking is completely out of the question. Simply standing, in and of itself, is a challenge. Walking? With a dog? Perish the thought.

But let's go back to waking up feeling good. That is often where we, as addicts, start re-writing our stories. We wake up. Maybe we hit a recovery meeting, go to church, or have coffee with friends or other addicts.

We start to put the pieces back together ... maybe get a job or actually start working at the job we managed to keep. We realize this whole recovery thing is do-able, working, and—dare I say it—worth it. It's not so bad. It's actually easier than anticipated. (And it can seem that way once the detox phase is over. During that, death often sounds like a welcome distraction.)

To me, this is one of the most dangerous times in the recovery journey. As alcoholics and addicts (and it's really one and the same), we become masters of re-writing our own collective realities. We make an art form of lying, manipulating, and fooling. We tend to forget (or overlook: we're also masters there) that *we* can also be victims of our incredible ability to manipulate and masquerade.

We start to think we're better.

> I WILL ALWAYS BE AN ALCOHOLIC, AS MUCH AS I WILL ALWAYS BE A BLUE-EYED MIDWESTERNER WITH A PREDISPOSITION TO LIGHT SENSITIVITY.

If you get one thing from this little read and one thing only, let it be this: We do not get better, and we do not get cured, though some rehab institutions out west would lead you to believe differently. We are, by the very nature of our fascinating and oddly wired brains, pre-disposed to always want to be altered, feel buzzed, and escape. We can learn to live with our addictions and live quite fabulously. Not one of us can ever pick up again, though, without playing our own little version of Russian Roulette. I, for one, don't want to take that risk today. Today, I will, with the help of my God, choose not to drink.

Is my life better than it was while I was drinking? Without question. Is my relationship with my family and friends better with me sober? Undoubtedly and absolutely. Do I enjoy my life more without the chains of my addiction weighing me down endlessly? Yes, and yes.

Am I better off? I am, I assure you.

Am I better? No. I am still an alcoholic. I will always be an alcoholic, as much as I will always be a blue-eyed Midwesterner with a predisposition to light sensitivity.

Let me repeat this. *We do not get cured of our addictions.* We can, as many twelve-step programs say, get a daily reprieve from the desire to drink or use.

Will I wake up tomorrow craving a big slice of chocolate cake with a glass of milk for breakfast? Probably not, I'm guessing. The sugar crash alone steers me away from doing such a thing. Do I know, though, that I won't wake up craving that very thing this coming Friday? I don't. I can't know until I wake up Friday morning. That's something for another day. I'll deal with it on that day to the best of my ability (though heaven knows having cake and milk for breakfast won't kill me, as my drinking quite probably could have and will do if I ever choose to do it again).

Today, I feel better. I must be hyper-aware, though, of feeling like I *am* better. It's not the doom and gloom it might seem. It doesn't center on my every thought anymore, though at first, it did. I can set myself up to have a good today by making good choices and by taking care of myself, much like a diabetic can feel good today by monitoring his or her diet and insulin levels. Is the diabetic still a diabetic on days he or she feels like a million bucks? You bet. Am I still an alcoholic on days I'm living like a normal person, going to work, cleaning my house, talking to friends?

I most certainly am.

Am I living on the *pink cloud* you hear others in recovery talking about? That place where everything starts to go right, you feel fantastic, things are working out, and nothing can get you down? Nope. For me, the pink cloud is pretty to look at, but once you start stepping on it, you realize it's simply an illusion. You might keep your balance for a bit, but eventually, you're going to hit a weak spot and poof! Down you fall.

The *pink cloud* was the reason I relapsed. I felt good. No, that's incorrect. I felt *great*! I was doing exactly what I had been told to do: hitting lots of meetings, taking care of myself, working with my sponsor, and relying on my HP. (Higher Power, and for those who don't know what an HP is, it can be anything: God, a tree, the universe, their recovery group, or whatever they feel gives them strength. It can't be another human being because humans can, and will, fail you.) I was getting what resembled a normal life back. I had managed to keep my job (thanks to a boss who should be nominated for sainthood, but that's a whole other book), I was rebuilding my relationships, and I was feeling *great*.

You know what? Most normal people don't go day to day feeling *great*. Most normal people will feel good one day, not so good the next, okay the third, pretty darn good the fourth, and so on. Feeling *great* is not realistic. It is not normal. And it will quite potentially lead to feeling better or cured, neither of which is possible.

For me, my *pink cloud* meant I had gotten it all wrong. I wasn't an alcoholic! Indeed, I'd only hit a rough patch, made some bad choices, and ended up in detox and rehab. It was a fluke. I mean, I was thankful for all of the help I'd received, and I was incredibly thankful for feeling normal again, but all those people had gotten it wrong too. Others had meant well, and at the time, I was feeling so shitty I would have done anything to feel better. Getting sobered up had been what I'd needed. I *was* better, though, and to celebrate (and prove) that, I was going to drink. Only a little. Because I was better!

Does anyone think that sounds familiar or like a good idea? Yeah. Not so much.

Within a day, I was back on the merry-go-round, but there was nothing merry about it. Once again, the compulsion to drink was there. The dragon was awake, and he was ready to rumble.

I am one of the lucky ones. My relapse was extremely brief, thanks in large part to the amazing people in my life: my friend Dave (who was also my boss), my incredible family, and my sponsor at the time, who has since gone back out. (That means she's no longer involved in recovery. I love her dearly and wish her well. We all walk our own path in our addictions and recovery.)

Some say relapse is a part of recovery. I don't like that saying. Relapse *can* be a part of recovery, as it was a part of mine, but it doesn't have to be. Again, like saying, "Being sober goes against our nature as addicts and alcoholics," doesn't give us the excuse *not* to work to stay clean and sober (and it *is* work), saying "Relapse is a part of recovery," does not give anyone license to go back out for a final

> AND TODAY, I AM DOING WHAT I NEED TO DO TO STAY SOBER.

yahoo. I know of many, many people who got clean and have stayed clean. I also know of many who've been in and out of recovery so fast and so many times it would make your head spin. Today, I am sober. It took a brief relapse for me to really get it. I understand that now, and I'm grateful I was able to get back on my program quickly. It doesn't mean I'll be sober tomorrow, though. I pray I will. I will work for it. All I have, in the grand scheme of things, is right now. Today. And today, I am doing what I need to do to stay sober.

Summary? Work to walk in the middle of the road. Do what it takes to keep yourself balanced: extremes, good or bad, will threaten your sobriety, especially in that crucial first few months. Feeling *too good* is not too good.

3

HOW IN THE HELL
DID I GET HERE?

Right before I hit the fast, downward spiral when my alcoholism truly took over, my life had become full of chaos and disarray. I was going through what was proving to be a very ugly breakup, and my soon-to-be-ex was doing all he could to make my days exceedingly difficult, disrupting what he could when he could. I had started a new job, which was good but stressful; I was attempting to sort through all of the bills I had discovered were owed, many past due, virtually all in my name alone (another outcome of the failed relationship); and my emotions and mindset were extremely fragile and unsettled.

I look back now and see how all the things I was experiencing set me up for a full-blown crash. As I attempted to sort everything out, more and more things I needed to attend to would be added to the mix. The more I discovered I needed to do to clean up the aftermath of the relationship, the more overwhelmed I became, and the more I wanted to escape it all. I drank to escape.

I can look back at my drinking history now and see red flags all over the place. With the exception of a few very close friends and family members, I had never felt I really fit in anywhere (this too is very common in those with addictions). I would often drink more than others around me to ease that feeling. I looked to drinking as a reward. I looked forward to going out, not only because it would be a chance to see others and be social, but also because it would afford me the opportunity to really let my hair down—to drink a good amount and not seem out of place or unusual. In the two years right before my spiral down, I began drinking in secret or drinking prior to going out.

My home life was not good. My partner had a sporadic employment history at best and was once again unemployed. Our house was tiny, much too small for two people, three dogs, and two cats to co-exist without stepping all over each other. I was living with a narcissistic addict and was experiencing a lot of abuse, most of it emotional and psychological, though at the time I wasn't aware of it. I only knew I felt bad about myself, my life, and my situation. I felt trapped, but my self-esteem was so low I felt helpless to do anything to change it. I was anxious, unsettled, and restless, and I didn't know how to deal with it. I did know drinking had always made me feel better, though, so I began to rely on that to deal with the *stuff* I was feeling.

My drinking became a hot topic between my partner and myself. I won't go into the details of my increasing dependence on drinking, but I will tell you I soon found myself needing it more and more often. What is important to note is I had all of the factors in place to feed my alcoholic brain and to fool it into thinking what I was doing was an acceptable way to deal with all I was feeling and experiencing in my life. I was restless, anxious, full of self-doubt, lost, unhappy, and in an extremely unhealthy relationship. I was, in a sense, heading toward the perfect storm.

My descent into full-blown alcoholism was swift and furious. I had been sliding down the slope for many years, but in the end, it only took a few short months for me to go from drinking wine (more and more of it) in the evening to drinking primarily vodka, virtually 24/7. I couldn't deal with what I was going through and ended up running directly into a bottle to escape it. My bottom lasted for about five months, all told, and at the end of those five months, I finally agreed to go to an inpatient treatment center. Rehab. It was the best single decision I've ever made in my life, and I am thankful beyond words to my family for not giving up on me and for continuing to press me to go … especially my sister. She was as tenacious as a little terrier, and I finally said I'd go to shut her up. My word, was I pissed.

(Thank you, Kate. From the bottom of my gratitude-filled heart: thank you.)

4

KEEP IT SIMPLE

One of the things I found most crucial to my recovery was, and is, to keep things simple. Simplify your schedule, simplify your surroundings, and simplify your life.

That is often much easier said than done.

AGAIN, AS ADDICTS, WE DON'T REALLY KNOW HOW TO FUNCTION EARLY ON WITHOUT WORRYING.

For me, it started in rehab. I (again) am one of the lucky ones. My parents said if I agreed to go to treatment, they would pay for it. What a precious, immeasurable gift that was, though I didn't fully know it at the time.

Schedules play a very large part in treatment once you're able to be up and about. Again, I was blessed.

Some very dear friends took care of me the few days it took to secure a bed at the facility, and I was able to enter treatment as sober as a newborn babe. This felt like both a blessing and a curse. I was alert and aware, which caused me to fully experience the terror of knowing I was going to rehab. It woke up every bit of anxiety I carried with me, and it was singing a chorus. Soon enough after being admitted, though, I could tell I was in a place of safety, where people really wanted to help me get better. Even with that, it took several days for me to stop playing happy and get down to the business of getting healthy.

Rehab serves several purposes. It helps us detox safely from our substance of choice, and it begins forming the framework we need to start healing with counseling, therapy, and classes so we can begin the interesting journey called recovery.

When Googling recovery, I found two definitions provided by the Oxford Dictionary that sum up the word beautifully as it relates to addiction.

1. A return to a normal state of health, mind, or strength.

2. The action or process of regaining possession or control of something stolen or lost.

(Personally, I prefer definition number two, even though my health and normalcy were neither stolen nor lost. I gave them away.)

Although I use the word *normal* a lot in this writing, I don't really know how to define it. For me, normal describes everyone who isn't suffering from a disease, either of the body or mind. That encompasses a whole lot. Also, as an alcoholic, I had to surrender my will and sense of control when I first began working my program of recovery, but I've learned since then I have a small modicum of control, and that makes me feel empowered. I can control my choices. I can control my decisions. I can control what I feel are the priorities in my life and my attention to them. In realizing that, I've found my own new normal.

Attending a twenty-eight-day recovery program allowed me to pare things down to the barest of bare. All I needed to worry about was me. I was reminded of that time and time again. I did, of course, worry about other things, though there was no need or reason to. Again, as addicts, we don't really know how to function early on without worrying.

I am blessed to be surrounded by an amazing family and amazing friends. The latter had arranged for my two dogs to be cared for in my absence, and my wonderful neighbors cared for my two kitties. They all reminded me I needed the time to start the process of healing so I could fully be there for my fuzzy kids. (Once again, I owe a debt I can only repay by living my life responsibly, helping where I can, and paying it forward.)

Rehab teaches you why you're so sick and how to evaluate whether or not you're willing to do the work it takes to get better. All that is asked is for the patients (and yes, you are not a guest or a customer: you are sick, so you're a patient) to attend classes and counseling sessions each day. After living for some time in chaos and despair, it was a huge relief to turn things over and do as I was asked to do. It didn't take long for them to see through my *happy*, either, and call bullshit on it. Once I fully realized I didn't have to perform like a dancing bear for anyone there, that indeed I was being asked *not* to, things began to happen.

Each day began with breakfast followed by chapel services for those who cared to attend, then a break, and after that, a meeting to announce the day's schedule. Each day was pretty much like the others with the only differences being who was scheduled for a one-to-one with their counselor or chaplain for the day. Those meetings were once or twice a week and were sometimes things to be looked forward to and sometimes not. (Have I mentioned recovery is not for the faint of heart?) After that, there were morning lectures, lunch, group therapy, usually another lecture, and then dinner. The evenings were often ours to do with as we pleased, and sometimes we attended twelve-step meetings off campus. Even so, the days were quite similar, and it was easy to develop a routine.

Again, a routine or a schedule is an imperative thing to have in recovery, especially in the early days. Unscheduled time and open days can be dangerous, even deadly. As addicts and alcoholics, our brains are wired differently, and as I mentioned earlier, it is unnatural for us to be clean and sober. An open block of time is easily transformed into a reason to be bored or restless. That, in turn, is easily turned into a reason to use. See why schedules and routines are so important?

YOUR RECOVERY IS GOING TO BE YOUR MOST IMPORTANT JOB FOR THE FORESEEABLE FUTURE; TREAT IT AS SUCH.

Establishing a routine is simple. Even if your work schedule varies from day to day, as mine has for a good part of my recovery, you can keep your days scheduled to some degree.

I've listed a few tips to help with that, and here they are:

* Establish a fairly consistent bedtime that works for most or all days and don't let it vary by more than an hour to an hour and a half.

* If your work schedule is consistent, schedule recovery meetings or counseling sessions into most days of the week. It is critical to immerse yourself in what you need to be doing in your early sobriety. This forms the foundation for living each day clean and sober if you choose to do so. Don't use money as an excuse to skip this. Whether you work a twelve-step program or not, anyone with a drinking or drug problem is welcome at meetings, there is no charge, and you can get an amazing amount of assistance and information simply by listening. Also, don't try the old "But I can't find any meetings where I live!" excuse. They're everywhere, and if there isn't one physically close to you, there are always online or phone meetings. If you want to get better, you'll find a solution that works for you.

* If your work schedule varies from day to day, find meetings or activities centered around

recovery that work for each day. Make showing up for your meetings as much of a priority as showing up for work. Your recovery is going to be your most important job for the foreseeable future; treat it as such.

* Make communication with family and friends who are supportive of your recovery a priority as well. Communicate with them every day, if possible. During my early sobriety, I composed bedtime and morning e-mails to my Dad, brother, and sister. This served two purposes: it let them know I was safe, sober, and okay; and it helped keep me tuned in to the important things in my life. That little habit has turned into a routine we all enjoy a great deal, and I feel it's helped me get to know each of them on a whole different level. Now, it's only me, my brother, and my sister sending morning e-mails, but I still look forward to both sending and receiving those e-mails every single day. I will forever be thankful I had the opportunity to do that with my Dad too.

* Plan meals and snacks to have throughout the day. Do not let yourself get too hungry or too thirsty; those can both be very detrimental.

There is an acronym in recovery known as H.A.L.T. It stands for hungry, angry, lonely, tired. If you feel restless, HALT and evaluate how you're feeling. Take immediate steps to correct it. It's exceedingly simple, yet it can work wonders.

* Schedule some *you* time in your week. Initially, there won't be a whole lot of time left over if you're working your program correctly, but it is important to take the time to chill out. Make sure you schedule your activity for that time as well. Go enjoy that Indian buffet you've been wanting to try, see a movie (or watch one at home), or take a nap. Knowing what you're going to do in your downtime is as important as having the rest of your time scheduled, particularly in the early days.

5

THE TOUGHEST
THING FOR ME

Looking back on my *personal adventures*, as my twelve-step program refers to it, the single hardest thing I had to do was admit I was an alcoholic and realize I needed to stop daydreaming about a day when I could ever again have a simple glass of wine. I can't—not if I want to continue my recovery process. It's incredibly important to pull yourself back to reality if you find yourself entertaining thoughts of drinking socially again or sharing some pills with a buddy before going out. This goes back to what was brought up earlier: we *can* drastically improve the quality of life each of us experiences, and we *can* make daily choices that will soon become habits that will give us a daily reprieve from the disease of addiction. We cannot, however, be cured of the disease of addiction or completely recover from it. That's why you could meet someone who has been sober twenty-five years who will still refer to him or herself as in recovery. We don't become recovered. It is a daily, lifelong process.

Once I was finally able to get over the idea of a long, long line of days ahead without a sip of wine or a cold beer on a hot day as an eventual possibility, things became much easier. Many recovery programs refer to this as surrendering, and it is a vital part of the recovery process. It makes sense it's such a hard thing to do; alcohol or drugs become the most important thing in an addict's life when the addiction is fully active. They are considered as crucial to living as air. That need is both physical and mental, and it will take time to surrender to the fact that it cannot be a part of life anymore if any semblance of a life is going to continue.

It is both fascinating and amazing to me how much life there is to be lived that doesn't involve any mind-altering substances at all and how many people (both recovering addicts and normal people) not only enjoy such a life but also suck the very marrow out of its bones. To put it very simply and bluntly, there is a hell of a lot of life to be lived without booze, pills, or drugs. There

> WE DON'T BECOME RECOVERED. IT IS A DAILY, LIFELONG PROCESS.

are endless possibilities of things to do, places to go, and people to see. There are groups for virtually any interest a person might have, from gardening to coin collecting to video gaming to writing, dancing, rescuing animals, learning Czechoslovakian while knitting. You name it; you can find it.

If you set your mind to it, that is.

6

GET UGLY HONEST

If you are 100% committed to your recovery, you *can* make things better. You *can* live a life so full and rich it can make your head spin. You can develop relationships that are deeper, more honest, and more fulfilling than you could ever have dreamed. You can create a new reality where you're not afraid, anxious, or looking for the dark shadows lurking in the corners.

To embark on this journey, though, you must get ugly honest. *Ugly honest* is a phrase I heard time and time again while I was in rehab. Ugly honest is exactly what it sounds like.

According to the Oxford Dictionary, the word *ugly* comes from an Old Norse word, *uggligr*, which translates into "to be dreaded." Honesty means (again, courtesy of Oxford) "free of deceit, truthful, and sincere." Ugly honest means taking a step back and looking at what you've done as a result of your disease and what that disease has done to you. It means being completely, 100% accountable for everything you said and did. It means you can't address most of your actions; you need to look at each and every one. Ugly honest involves delving into your past to figure out what might have contributed to your addiction: childhood abuse, mental issues or illness, genetics, a psychological trauma … the list goes on and on. It means looking at exactly what you've done to people you love. It means turning over each stone and examining its underbelly for whatever might lie there. It means waking up, growing up, and finally taking responsibility for yourself, your actions, addiction, and life.

> IF YOU STAY, YOU MIGHT DIE. IF YOU LEAVE, YOU MIGHT NOT.

Being ugly honest is hard. It's mentally exhausting, painful, and brings up all the feelings I now associate with my end drinking days … the feelings I drank more because of in the hopes of shutting them down, shutting them up. It creates anxiety, worry, heartache, anger, and regret. It is painful in a way I've never felt pain before because it's an emotional pain. It's imperative to feel that pain and work through it, though. It does hurt to re-live all those emotions, and it's harder than hell to take a head-on look at the wreckage you've made of your life, but if you can't take that long, hard look, you won't be able to start repairing the damage or healing from the issues. You might be able to stop drinking or using for a while, and you might even find yourself on a pink cloud, but all of those hurts, shortcomings, and faults will still be there below the surface, waiting for the right moment to pop out. And they will pop out. You might not realize it until you've already taken your first or second hit or you've polished off the pint, but they'll sit patiently, and all of a sudden, they'll be marching in front of you like a mariachi band in a parade, trumpeting and braying and saying "Hello! Miss us? Here we are, and look at you … just like old times! So glad you're back. How about you stay a while?"

You might choose to leave the parade, or you might decide to sit and watch it for a bit. Hell, you might even decide to pick up an instrument and join in the march. If you stay, you might die. If you leave, you might not.

If you are unwilling or unable to become ugly honest, find someone who can and will help you find that strength. It could be a friend, sponsor, pastor, or therapist. It is one of the keys to this whole recovery journey. This key might fight back when you try to turn it, and it might cause you to break a sweat, utter some really offensive words, or even have to put up a righteous battle, but the key will eventually turn. If you keep working it, I promise you that key will turn, and it will open the door to a life you could never have imagined.

7

NOT EVERY STORY HAS A
HAPPY ENDING

There are a lot of realities associated with recovery. Some of those realities are beautiful things and are cause for a whole lot of joy. There could be the reality of a great new job at which you can excel. It could be the reality of a relationship with your family that is honest, genuine, and truly enriching. It could be the reality of paying your bills on time and of being responsible and dependable. It could be a whole lot of really good stuff.

It could also be some not so good stuff. For some, this new reality involves court cases, judges, and jail time. For others, it involves an overwhelming amount of debt needing to be addressed and repaid. It might involve being on the receiving end of a lot of anger from friends and family you've hurt deeply and who are still feeling the pain of their endless worry (and believe you me, even if you think your addiction didn't hurt anyone but you, you are assuredly and sorely mistaken).

My story involved a mix of the two. I am incredibly thankful to have not had more legal issues to deal with, aside from a DUI that was a huge part of my bottom, but that also ended up being one of the greatest blessings of my life. Were it not for that DUI and the restrictions and financial toll that followed, I might have not only gone back out but also gone back out in my party dress, noisemaker in one hand, drink in the other. Were it not for that damn interlock device in my car (it's now gone, but when I had it, I chose to be thankful every time I had to blow in it to start it up and each time I had to take a rolling re-test), I could have taken the easy way out and stopped by a liquor store when things got a bit too tough to handle. Were it not for the daily phone calls I had to make to see if I'd be summoned for a random u/a the next day, I might have slipped when slipping could have caused me to tumble to my death. Were it not for the little green slips of paper I had to turn in at my monthly appointments with my P.O., I might not have developed the habit of attending regular twelve-step meetings. Were it not for a lot of things that happened, I could be spoken of and about only in the past tense today. Of that, I am certain. Maybe it wouldn't have happened yet, but

I know either by the toll of alcohol on my body and organs or by my own hand, ensconced in the darkness and despair where a person resides in true, desperate and hopeless addiction, I would eventually have wound up dead. That thought now makes me shudder. Quite frankly, knowing how close I came to taking my own life to escape the torment and pain of my alcoholism scares the hell out of me. I do know it, though, and by the grace of God, I didn't do it.

Others aren't so lucky.

Addiction is a disease. It is a disease of the body and mind, and it digs deep, deep, deep. Part of the reason both addiction and mental illness are often scoffed at, or brushed off with a simple, "Well, she could just stop drinking/using/cutting if she really wanted to," is the fact that you don't really see the disease itself, only the behaviors and consequences of it. Others see it as being a disease relegated to street people, crazy people, and lazy and irresponsible people. To non-addicts, it seems like a simple problem of self-control, but it's not. It goes so much deeper than that, and addiction is a ridiculously patient bastard. It sits quietly in wait, and it can pop up anytime, anywhere. Once the physical symptoms begin to present themselves, it's often too late.

I know of several people who went through the same treatment program I did who aren't around anymore. I didn't know them personally, but I feel they are kindred souls. It shows me how very serious my disease is. Many of these people were on good paths in their recovery and were not even considered as people who might relapse. The same might be said for those involved in solid programs of recovery who then decided to test the waters again, so to speak. Some are still out there, and I keep them in my heart and prayers. Some might be dead, but I may not know it yet. Others soon will be if they stay out. Others will live on, but the lives they're living are riddled with pain, uncertainty, and fear because they're not ready or willing to choose a new path.

> ADDICTION IS A DISEASE. IT IS A DISEASE OF THE BODY AND MIND, AND IT DIGS DEEP, DEEP, DEEP.

Some of these addicts will get back on their feet again. Some will keep going through the revolving door: into treatment, back to using, into detox, and back out again. It is not a matter of sheer willpower when it comes to addiction. Discipline is crucial in a solid program of recovery, and it's part of what is learned early in the recovery process, but sheer will only holds out so long before the voices start piping up again. Without taking 100% accountability for his or her own recovery, it's only a matter of time before someone is drunk or high again, and then all bets are off.

8

THE MOST IMPORTANT THINGS I'VE LEARNED TO HELP KEEP ME SOBER

I often think of questions I asked early in my recovery, and I still hear them when I help take a meeting to a detox facility or rehab center. Some of the most common questions are, "What is the most important thing to do in recovery?" and "When will it get better?" Here are my attempts to answer both of those questions as I have learned on my own journey.

"What is the most important thing to do in recovery?"

My answer to this question is a two-parter. The turning points for me were complete surrender and reliance on a power greater than myself to help me through things when I didn't have the strength on my own to go one more step.

1. Complete surrender is an action I believe to be absolutely critical to having a successful journey of recovery. I have noticed those who harbor any residual thoughts of *just one more time* are already beginning a relapse. It simply hasn't happened ... yet. If there is a nuance, glimmer, or trace of thought about drinking or using again, chances are quite good that person will drink or use again unless he or she takes that thought, faces it head-on, surrenders once more, and keeps making good choices.

> I BELIEVE ONCE SURRENDER IS ACCEPTED AT THE CORE OF YOUR HEART AND SOUL, RECOVERY TRULY BEGINS.

Here is the caveat: you can completely surrender once or one thousand times. Complete surrender can be a mindset obtained once at the beginning of recovery for some and can be a daily part of recovery for others. It doesn't matter how often surrender must be done as long as it *is* done. If an addict can keep the knowledge that he or she is powerless when it comes to alcohol or drugs, he or she can move on to other things. It takes work, practice, and being present mentally and emotionally. It hurts sometimes, and it can create a sense of grief and loss and a raw and open wound that feels as if it won't ever heal. It might have to be revisited fifty times an hour in the first few days or weeks of being clean and sober, but if it is approached honestly and with purpose and intent, it will start to stick.

I believe once surrender is accepted at the core of your heart and soul, recovery truly begins. Keep at it. It took quite some time for me, but I eventually got it. On the rare occasions the thought of a drink enters my noggin, I revisit where it got me before. I play my tape all the way through, I re-commit and surrender once more, and I get on my knees and pray for strength, giving thanks for my sobriety. (I always make sure to give thanks for all I've been so blessed to receive.)

2. A spiritual connection to and reliance on something greater than you (often referred to as a Higher Power.)

I've noticed a common theme in those who are in successful programs of recovery: a strong spiritual center. For most, but not all, that spiritual center (or Higher Power) is God. I know it's most certainly God for me.

I am very fortunate because I've always had a strong spiritual side. I was raised in the church, and despite all they did there, I maintained my faith. (I'm not a big fan of organized religion, but there again is a whole other book.) My connection to God is something I don't remember developing or working on; it's always been there. It's interesting too because I've always felt very connected to God but not so much to Jesus. I didn't realize that until I was well into my program of recovery, but I took that as another sign I was in the right program for me.

I've come to learn faith is like a muscle. The more you exercise it, the stronger it grows. It hurts a bit sometimes, and it can feel like you're working it and working it, and nothing ever happens, and then, bam! One day, you'll realize you've got a little something there. It's getting stronger, and that in turn makes you work it a little more. It's what I refer to as a snowball rolling uphill: it will continue to grow and expand and move you to a better and better place.

Some might have their spiritual connection to the universe and to the energy there. Others might find nature itself to be their spiritual place. It does not matter what your connection is to something greater than you; the important thing is you *do* have a connection to something. For some who attend support and recovery groups, it is the group itself. The only thing it cannot be is one single person. People might have intentions that are true and wonderful, but people can fail, and any sort of failure can be seen as a reason to drink or to use. Don't set yourself up for that (and if you are setting yourself up for that, go back to the surrender part).

My faith has grown in leaps and bounds in my recovery, and with that faith in my God comes a huge sense of relief. I can take the pressure off my own shoulders and concentrate on doing what I know is right and making good and healthy choices. As long as I keep doing that, things seem to be working out.

Things will continue to work out toward your better good if you practice both surrender and reliance on something greater than yourself. There will be times it doesn't seem things are working out as you'd like them to, and that's probably true. We don't necessarily know what's best for us. If we did, why would we be in recovery in the first place? Turn things over and know as long as you're doing your part, they're working out exactly as they're supposed to.

"When will it get better?"

This is the million-dollar question. There isn't a set answer. I'm sorry if you were hoping for one; there's not. The only thing I can promise is it *will* get better if you keep at the things you're supposed to be doing.

As with many things recovery-related, one often doesn't realize things are getting better until they *are* better. I distinctly remember waking up one day, realizing I didn't want to drink. I hadn't, in fact, even been obsessing over it as I had been doing for the previous year or so. I ruminated on that for a while and finally started to cry, both with relief and the overwhelming feeling of being freed. I think about that turning point quite often. I didn't realize it was coming, but I was attending recovery meetings, counseling sessions, group therapy, and taking care of my day-to-day obligations such as my fuzzy kids, their needs, my job, and financial responsibilities. I was doing what I was supposed to be doing, and it was hard and painful and exhausting, and my HP must have realized that and decided to offer me a taste of why I was doing what I was doing. There was the start of that uphill snowball. I realized what I was doing was working, by golly, and that made me dig my heels in deeper and want to do it more, and better, and with greater conviction.

> I WAS DOING WHAT I WAS SUPPOSED TO BE DOING, AND THINGS WERE GETTING BETTER.

I remember very clearly sitting at a detox center as a patient. That was my first of two detoxes, and it was a frightening experience. It started to hammer home how very serious my situation was and how deeply entrenched I was in my alcoholism. A local recovery group came one evening to bring a meeting to the center and share their message with us. I remember sitting there, listening to their stories, thinking to myself, *there is no way these people were as bad or as desperate as I am right now.* I remember being grateful they took the time to come and being so angry with them because they all seemed to radiate a sense of peace. I remember feeling a strong rush of despair, hopelessness, and loneliness. I remember thinking to myself that if I could ever get better, I wanted to be one of them—to be sitting in the chairs reserved for the people who chose to come to this place and who got to go home when they were done.

I'm now able to help others struggling with their addictions by taking meetings to detox and rehabilitation centers. I'm blessed to be able to do that. Each time I do, I bring up that memory, and I tell them how incredibly, immeasurably thankful I am to be able to come share some of what I know with them and to be able to go home when we're done. I realize it pisses some of them off, and that's okay; being pissed at those people when I was in detox was part of what inspired me to keep working on my own healing. If they get mad at me and it helps one of them knuckle down and get to work, it's worth it.

The first time I visited a detox, and I got up to walk out the door, get in my car, and drive myself home was when it was knocked into my strangely-wired brain that yes, indeed, things were getting better. I was doing what I was supposed to be doing, and things were getting better. I was working hard, I was being ugly honest, I was pushing myself to feel the discomfort, pain, and emotions I had been running from for most of my life, but it was finally starting to happen.

Things will get better. When? I don't know—not for you. I only know if you do your part, it will come. That's part of the whole *faith in something greater than yourself* too.

9

WHY IS CONNECTION TO A HIGHER POWER ESSENTIAL?

I gradually came to the realization the people I was seeing who were not successful in recovery had a commonality, and that was a lack of a spiritual connection to something bigger than they were or are. I began to wonder about that. How could it be that a lack of faith in something could keep people from staying sober and clean? I mean, bottles, pipes, and needles are solid, tangible things. How could it be that faith, which is not solid, touchable, or tangible, might be the single greatest factor in keeping some people in recovery and keeping others in active addiction?

I've come up with a couple of theories, and for me, the spiritual connection comes first because again, for me, God can provide the strength, insight, patience, and knowledge that things are all working toward a bigger good—for you, your loved ones, and your life.

SUSAN'S THEORY #1: THERE MUST BE SOMETHING BIGGER THAN YOU

Without a spiritual connection, true serenity cannot be found, and serenity and the fierce protection of it are what will help you to keep making the right choices, and it is a critical part of keeping you sober.

I've had to go to court on several occasions to deal with bills that were not being tended to by someone I was once involved with. According to him, circumstances were keeping him from being responsible. Whatever reason he invented, that wasn't the imperative issue. The most important thing I needed to do was to stay focused, present, strong, and spiritually fit. I went to my meetings, said a lot of prayers, kept in contact with my family and friends, and made it through everything successfully. I felt as though I was constantly asking God for help. Help with anxiety. Help with fear. Help with the unknown. Help to guide me in making the right choices and doing the hard things that needed to be done.

He helped me through it, and I did not drink.

My Dad, who had been an astronomically-important person in helping me recover, died quite unexpectedly a bit less than two years into me being sober. My step-mom immediately had to be moved into an assisted care facility because he'd been her caretaker, and she wasn't able to live on her own. My sister had to handle the estate, and I helped clear the house, find a place for Mom and get her settled, and tie up loose ends.

I did not drink over it.

Weeks ago, I had to say goodbye to my constant, my friend, my source of comfort and unconditional love: my sweet fuzzy kid, Desmond. He not only helped me more than I can ever express in my recovery, but he was also there every day before and after. He was in my heart when I was in treatment, helping me work to heal and get better so I could be the best mom to my four-legged children I could possibly be. He was there when my Dad died: big head in the door, tail wagging, body wiggling, ready to be my confidant, my biggest cheerleader, a soft blanket for my tears, and my source of joy and laughter and love. We had some wonderful days right before, and his departure was peaceful, quiet, and filled with love and comfort. The loss of him almost ripped me in two. I've never felt pain like the pain I've experienced in my grief over the loss of my best friend. I can't tell you the number of times I've wailed and fallen to my knees, asking God to help me through the next few minutes because I was absolutely certain I couldn't handle the emotional pain of that loss. Give me a broken leg, a broken back, a broken foot: those I can handle. Pain that cannot be touched or tended to in any way other than letting it out is frightening in its intensity and power. I know the outpouring of grief and loss was about more than losing him, and I knew I had to feel it, touch it, taste it, and own it, and it would eventually pass. I'm crying now as I write this because that pain still exists. It's ebbed a bit, and when it comes, it passes more quickly. I know now it will pass, so I can more easily let it come.

I chose not to drink.

I'm lucky. Because of my relationship with my father, especially in regards to my recovery, to have slipped after he died would have been like slapping him in the face while saying, "Fuck you." I would no sooner choose to do that to my Dad than I would choose to cut off my own leg. Knowing how proud he was of the strides I'd made and how much closer we had grown through the struggles ... well, that was something I didn't want to tarnish by taking a drink. Even more than that, though, with the loss of Dad and then of Desi, I went back to talking to God constantly, endlessly. "God, help me get out of bed. God, help me be strong. God, help me make it through the next fifteen minutes, the next hour, this day. God, please just help."

PAIN THAT CANNOT BE TOUCHED OR TENDED TO IN ANY WAY OTHER THAN LETTING IT OUT IS FRIGHTENING IN ITS INTENSITY AND POWER.

Letting God handle the things I'm unable to handle has helped me get through the losses of two of the most important individuals in my life without drinking, and He continues to help me because I'm still working through the grief. Trusting that He has my back and knowing the feelings and emotional pain *will pass*, has helped get me through. Talking to Him constantly and staying in the moment gives me the strength to make it each day. And that leads me to my next theory.

SUSAN'S THEORY #2: STAY IN THE MOMENT. BE PRESENT. ALWAYS.

For me, being present is also one of the hugest factors in staying sober. I find if I'm constantly in touch with God, I'm able to stay in the moment and take things as they come instead of planning for what's around the corner. As addicts, our brains are wired differently.

I know my brain will buy a ticket and ride that roller coaster until I'm puking uncontrollably, and when other people would go home, I'll get back in line for another go-round. If I don't reign in my thinking, stay connected to God, and stay in the moment, my mind will take me places that will not do me one lick of good. If I don't stay present, I've almost immediately set myself up for the pre-relapse way of thinking.

It's not easy.

Staying present requires a whole lot of practice, and for me, a whole lot of praying. Staying present requires a person to deal with what's real and what's happening at that moment. Again, as addicts, we see something unpleasant, and our first inclination is to run. Run to the liquor store. Run to the dealer. Run to the pharmacy for a refill. Run to get that *something*, that *anything* that will help us escape from the reality of whatever it is we're facing. It doesn't have to be big, either. It can be a bill that isn't paid. It can be an upcoming family gathering. It can simply be getting out of bed and walking out the door.

To stay present, at least for me, means to pray. A lot. I pray for strength, help, and release from anxiety. With the strength I find through prayer and through my Higher Power, I can stay present (most of the time, anyway). If you stay present, it forces you to see clearly what's real and what's in front of you. When you see clearly, eventually you'll figure out things are not always what you make them out to be. We usually make them a lot bigger than they are anyway because that gives us a reason to use. It's the way we're made.

Being present helps because it requires action. If you aren't constantly trying to avoid things, you have to deal with issues as they come up. (Yes, it sounds overly simplistic. It is. Addicts and alcoholics *love* to complicate matters by over-thinking them.)

Being present and staying present won't happen overnight. It's a learned way of living. It might start for you, as it did for me, with the almost constant realization I was looking beyond my *right now*, and I needed to pull back. Most of the time, I'd say a prayer for help with whatever it was that was causing me to jump ahead. I would get extremely angry at myself because of my inability to face the moment I was experiencing, but only by keeping myself in my now was I able to learn how much of my days were taken up by avoidance and plans of escape. It's similar to some people one might find in the workplace: some spend so much time trying to figure out how to get out of doing work that they don't realize if they did the job, it would be completed in no time at all. If I find myself looking for the exit door, I stop, take a deep breath, and figure out what is causing me to panic. More often than not it's something I can handle pretty easily, and by staying present, facing the task (or issue or problem or fear) and dealing with it, I decrease my anxiety, and I learn a little bit.

It's okay to daydream sometimes or think about things you wish you'd done differently. Give yourself a moment with the memory, thought, or daydream and then let it go and get right back to your now. It can be pretty tough at first and quite discouraging, but know each time you can make yourself stay present,

> BEING PRESENT AND STAYING PRESENT WON'T HAPPEN OVERNIGHT. IT'S A LEARNED WAY OF LIVING.

you're learning a new way to live, and that new way will help you stay clean and sober.

SUSAN'S THEORY #3: LET THE FEELINGS COME

My alcoholism is a result of several different things. One is a genetic predisposition to addiction. I have raging alcoholics in the good old family tree along with lots of addictive behaviors throughout (not necessarily to alcohol). There are several other factors too that came together over my several decades of living, and they gave my disease plenty of ammo.

I was diagnosed in my late thirties with post-traumatic stress disorder (PTSD) due to the death of my Mom when I was ten and some events that followed. I won't go into details here: I'll only say I learned people responded better if I shoved the bad shit down, smiled a lot, and didn't complain about things. By shoving bad shit down, smiling a lot, and not complaining, I became known over time as happy. Being known as happy puts a lot of pressure on a person not to be upset, angry, or sad, so I learned to associate those feelings as bad, and I locked them away.

As I mentioned at the beginning of this little book, everything is not always great. People are not always happy. It's virtually impossible to live in a constant state of up. Ying and yang, positive and negative, everything has a natural balance to it, and if that balance is not allowed to occur, one side will inevitably get over-burdened and will eventually give way.

I gradually learned I was a pretty happy drunk. When I was drinking, the little stuff kind of floated away, and I felt good. As my disease took hold, I started to believe I was more likable, more social, and better in general if I had a bit of alcohol to smooth my rough edges. I felt I was really being my authentic self when I was drinking. I laughed harder, I was bolder, and I was funnier. It was easier to stuff the bad shit down when I was drinking.

Well, the bad shit didn't want to stay down. That area was becoming too over-burdened, too full, and it needed to be released. It started to show itself (as it will) as it could, which was usually when I'd had much too much to drink. It came about as over-reactions, as hysterical crying fits, and at the bottom of my low, as thoughts and talk of suicide. When it finally came up, it came up so big, fierce, and strong I would stagger under the weight of it, and it would crush any happy I had.

One of the moments in my recovery I will remember as long as I'm on this side of the dirt happened when I was in treatment. Part of the course was a women's therapy group. It was during one of the first meetings I was called out on my happy.

There was another woman at the facility who did not like me. I now know it was because of my happy façade, which in hindsight, is almost comical. I was in a treatment center for alcoholism, scared half to death, surrounded by drunks, drug addicts, and people who were terrifically sick, sad, and broken, still pretending everything was okay, and I was fine.

She called me out on my bullshit.

I don't remember exactly how it started. We were in group, and we were going around sharing, and all of a sudden, I felt I was the recipient of a full-on attack. This particular woman began to berate me. I remember her pointing at me, almost in a rage, talking about how I always went around smiling and happy, and there was no *way* I was happy, and she was tired of it, and it was pissing her off.

I was stunned. I thought I'd been fooling everyone and hadn't given a second thought to the fact that I was now surrounded by people who lied to others and themselves all of the time and that those people were pros. They could see exactly what I was doing as she had done. She had the courage (or she was mad enough) to call me on it.

That was one of the moments I truly started to work on my own recovery. I began to talk, and I began to cry, and I remember another young woman looking at me with true concern in her eyes as she said, "Living like that must be exhausting."

That person calling me out, and the other woman acknowledging how tired I was, and trying to keep everyone around me happy released something in me. I know I realized it at the time as being a big moment, a life-changer, and I know in retrospect it was one of the most important moments in helping me start to heal.

Feeling is normal. Feeling is natural. The ability to emotionally feel is one of the most beautiful gifts we're given as evolved beings, and I believe my God put feelings in all of us because they make this whole living process much richer and more rewarding. We are beings of free will, thought, and emotion. To have believed I could keep it all one-sided, all positive, all good now makes me chuckle. To know I was fully capable of being sad, angry, or upset, but chose not to show those emotions makes me sad. I'm sad for the girl I was and for the woman I was, forcing her to live that way. It *is* exhausting, and the really sad thing is it was largely self-imposed.

> IT WAS EASIER TO STUFF THE BAD SHIT DOWN WHEN I WAS DRINKING.

Today, I let myself feel. Most days, I am pretty happy: it's the way I'm made, as I'm fond of telling people. I *know* and accept now, though, that I'm also very sensitive, I'm stubborn, and I get mad. I let those things out. I let those *feelings* out. I pray for God to put the right words in my mouth and for me to do according to His will and not my will, and I've gotten pretty adept at seeing when my will is creeping to the front of the line. Sometimes I say things I know might not be what others want to hear, but I know I need to say them, because otherwise, they'll get stuffed down, and they'll sit and start to fester, eventually bursting out, one way or another. I know if I don't let them out, they could cause me to want to drink again, and I don't want to do that. I don't need to do that if I make good choices and do what I know I should do.

One thing I need to do is to be real. To laugh loudly, get mad, and have days where I feel like crying, and I let the tears fall. It's still difficult sometimes. I still find crying strangely hard to do: I catch myself cutting the tears off, and that's not good for me. I find myself with anger welling inside, and the old Susan saying, "Oh, that is a bad thing!" and starting to stuff it down. The real me, the *authentic* me, overrides her and lets the anger come. It is so cathartic, as is all emotion allowed to flow without being deemed correct or incorrect, right or wrong. As with many things learned in recovery, I am learning how to control these emotions as they come to a certain degree, so they don't present themselves at completely inappropriate times (and they most certainly have done that since I started letting them out). I have learned and am continuing to learn when it's socially acceptable to be angry, sad, or upset and to what extremes. I'm learning, too, by being these things, feeling these things, and expressing these emotions, it does not make me a bad person. It makes me a whole person.

> IT IS SO CATHARTIC, AS IS ALL EMOTION ALLOWED TO FLOW WITHOUT BEING DEEMED CORRECT OR INCORRECT, RIGHT OR WRONG.

I have yet to find someone who shuns me because I'm not happy all the time. That is the complete opposite of exhausting. It's liberating.

10

WATCH OUT FOR THOSE WHO WON'T LET YOU FEEL

Having lived most of my life (including the majority of my adult life) thinking I had to be happy all the time naturally drew to me people who liked that quality and others who came to expect it. Others who, mired in their own addictions and issues, would not accept anything *but* the happy Susan.

If you have people like that in your life, give them a firm, swift kick in the ass and get them the hell out. Do not pass go, do not collect $200, do not buy a hotel. Get them gone. People like that will not only hinder your recovery, but they might also want to keep you in your active addiction, no matter how much they claim to want to help.

I had a person like that in my life. I can remember not feeling good one morning after I'd gotten up. I was feeling sad, and I didn't want to put on my happy. As soon as he saw me not smiling, he immediately said, "What's up, crabapple? Why are you so grumpy today?" As a matter of fact, I wasn't grumpy. I simply wasn't happy. I learned quickly in that relationship I wasn't allowed to be anything but happy. If I cried, I was "so oversensitive!" If I became frustrated or upset, I was "so emotional!" If I became angry, I was "so pissy!" This person became very involved in getting me better but refused to alter his behavior to help. Those around me heard ad nauseum, "She has these issues but refuses to get help. I'm not the bad guy here. I am reaching out to help her get the help she so desperately needs." In hindsight, he wanted me better on his terms. He wanted me to be the happy I was early in the relationship before it became controlling and abusive, but he also still wanted to be able to go out, watch football, drink, and have me stop when he told me to.

I now know I stayed in the relationship for far too long, but we're all on our own timeframe. Had I not stayed, would I have eventually found my way to my now? Would things have played out the way they did? I've heard many times in my recovery that "You got here exactly when you were supposed to." I might re-play the *what ifs*, but that doesn't serve any purpose.

I am here now. Maybe me saying this, though, is letting you know this is your *supposed to* time.

As alcoholics and addicts, we don't know what normal is, and that includes normal relationships. I'm not sure how much we learn from being around abnormal or unhealthy relationships and how much we create with our own minds, but I've met very few people who were in solid, grounded, and healthy relationships when they hit their bottoms. Virtually everyone who enters recovery can recall at least one instrumental relationship that was unhealthy, flawed, or broken. I think a big part of it is that our addictive minds don't see healthy relationships as normal. We are creatures of chaos, disorder, and extremes, and healthy can equal boring in our strangely-wired brains.

CONCENTRATE ON PEOPLE IN YOUR LIFE WHO WANT TO SEE YOU HEALTHY, WHO WANT TO SEE YOU BETTER.

Now that I'm approaching two years of recovery and sobriety, I see boring very differently: it's my wonderful new normal. I am enjoying living my days simply and somewhat predictably (though we all know nothing is ever truly predictable). I know I can't control the grand scheme of things, but I can control my choices and my actions for the most part, and that helps keep things simple. I can choose who I want to spend my time with and how I'd like to spend that time. I steer away from drama and chaos, finding joy in little things.

Concentrate on people in your life who want to see you healthy, who want to see you better. Focus on the people who love you no matter what and who aren't giving up on seeing you break free of this hellish thing we call addiction. Keep the people in your life who love you, warts and all, but want to see you clean and sober, and throw out the others without so much as a how do you do. They're toxic, they're dangerous, and as much as they insist they love you and they care, it's smoke and mirrors. They're not in the relationship for you but for their own selfish reasons, and trust me: they will take you down in flames if given the chance, but *they* will likely end up lightly seared at worst.

11

WHAT NOW?

I recently had to go back to court to resolve some issues from the above-mentioned old relationship. My Dad was still alive at the time, and I remember clearly telling him how upset I was because my serenity was being so adversely affected, and that made me extremely angry. I think Dad and I realized together at that moment how far I'd come that I was so fiercely protective of my peace of mind, and *realizing* that was a huge a-ha moment for both of us. I had come to relish the quiet days, the predictable days, the smooth days. They were outnumbering the days of disquiet and disorder, and that was a very good thing. It still is, even with the tough stuff that will inevitably pop up in the road. It's often referred to as "Life on life's terms." Once you can accept that, and you come to the realization you can face it, even with the upheavals it presents, life is pretty darn good.

I was sitting quietly a few days ago, chatting with God as I tend to do most mornings. I was thanking Him for my sobriety, and I began to reflect on the things happening in my life right now. The loss of my Dad and Desi are obviously the biggest things, and I'm dealing with those losses each day as best I can. There are a lot of other things happening too: having to put a parent in an assisted-care facility, as we had to do with my stepmom after the loss of Dad, and handling the things that go along with that (guilt, concern, relief, worry); going through a house stuffed full of memories and paring things down; watching my siblings deal with the loss of Dad in their own ways, and not being able to do anything to ease their pain but lend an ear or a shoulder; knowing my sweet kitties are in the autumn of their days as well (I often refer to my home as the geriatric home for wayward animals, and they're both sixteen, though many days, you wouldn't know it); trying to figure out if I stay where I am or move closer to my brother and sister, and always, always knowing I must remain fully committed to my recovery and everything that entails: well, I'd say my plate is kind of full right now.

Know what? It's the same thing as people saying they want to have a child, but it's not the right time. There rarely is a right time to have a child. It happens, you celebrate, and you get on with making it work.

There is rarely a right time to get into recovery, though addicts and alcoholics like to think differently. We think we'll have one more hurrah, one more night out, one more trip to the sun and back. What we don't think about is that *one more* could be the *one too many*, and that would monumentally suck.

I know of a lot of people who aren't here to read these words I've written down because they wanted that one more. Would reading this have helped any of them? I'm not self-absorbed enough to say yes, but I've learned enough to say maybe.

I've learned so much over the past two years, and the biggest life lesson I've received is this: everything we feel that isn't positive stems from fear. I am incredibly fearful writing about this. I'm fearful no one will read it, and I'm fearful everyone will. I start thinking of the responsibility I'm putting on my own shoulders by putting a little bit of my story out there, and that scares me to death, but then something stops me in my tracks.

What if I didn't put my experience out there, and it could have helped someone?

That thought, that *maybe* is enough for me to know I can do this. I also have faith knowing I'm being led to tell my story, and that helps me tremendously. I know in the recent past when I've made the right choices, things have tended to work out pretty well. That doesn't mean the results of the choices have been easy. At times, it's been hard as hell, and there have been days I've literally had to go moment to moment, falling on my knees in between, terrified of what might be next.

> WHAT WE DON'T THINK ABOUT IS THAT ONE MORE COULD BE THE ONE TOO MANY, AND THAT WOULD MONUMENTALLY SUCK.

I sit here now, knowing nothing that has happened has been harder to get through than my half-nutty brain makes the unknown out to be. That is, as long as I do my part, as long as I do the work, and as long as I stay real, focused, and spiritually connected. I'm not steel-plated and bullet-proof as many drunks and addicts believe themselves to be, but I am a whole hell of a lot stronger than I'd ever given myself credit for.

And for this day, for right now, for this Optimistic Drunk, that's enough.

How about you? Are you ready to make the decision to take your life back from the stranglehold of your addiction? Are you ready to make the choice to get clean, sober, healthy, and back into this thing we call living? It won't be a cakewalk. It will require brutal honesty, reaching down into the pit of your soul to pull out what's been festering there, and it will require leaning on others and leaning on something bigger than you: leaning on sheer faith and sheer will. It will tear you up and beat you down, and then it will re-build you so much stronger, so much better.

It is not easy. But again: my worst day sober is one hundred times better than my best day drunk. Taking a line from one of my favorite books and movies of all time, "Get busy living or get busy dying." Stop avoiding the responsibility that is yours. You're sick. If you want to get better, you can start right now. You can start. You.

It's *your* choice to make.

RESOURCES FOR ASSISTANCE

ALCOHOLICS ANONYMOUS

The tenets of AA have helped an untold number of people find a real, workable program to live by. I've often thought the world in general could benefit from the blueprint of AA (the Twelve Steps). Anyone is welcome at any time (many AA groups accept addicts of any type: some prefer to keep it to those who are proficient at abusing alcohol). There are no fees. If it's tough to get to a meeting, online meetings are an option, though there's nothing quite like experiencing first-hand the wisdom and support of a big group of drunks who've been sober for a few twenty-four-hour chunks. Bottom line: there is no excuse not to be able to get to regular AA meetings. They're everywhere.

https://www.aa.org/
888-486-0889

NARCOTICS ANONYMOUS

NA follows much of the same outline as AA, but different groups have different ways of operating. The primary difference is the focus on the addiction in NA, rather than the source of the addiction in AA. Some NA groups accept people whose drug of choice is alcohol, and some aren't as open. The key is trying out different meetings until you find one that feels like a good fit. Trust me: you'll know when you get there, and it's definitely worth the time to keep trying until you find that group.

https://www.na.org/
818-773-9999

VALLEY HOPE

Valley Hope is a treatment program with a presence in seven states, primarily in the Midwest. They offer programs for both alcohol and drug addiction and have a variety of rehabilitation programs, both inpatient and outpatient. They also offer financing for their programs.

https://valleyhope.org/
1-800-544-5101

NATIONAL SUICIDE PREVENTION HOTLINE

Many addicts are masking underlying emotional and/or mental problems or illnesses. We numb, self-medicate, and run. Sometimes the numbing or evading techniques don't work, and the shame, despair, and hopelessness run full-throttle. If you are feeling suicidal, or even contemplating taking your own life, please talk to someone. Call 911 if that's all you can muster the strength to do. The world needs you in it: don't let this hateful, horrible disease make you a statistic.

https://suicidepreventionlifeline.org
1-800-273-8255

EAP (EMPLOYEE ASSISTANCE PROGRAMS)

If you're employed, check to see if your employer offers an EAP. Many companies of all sizes offer some form of employee assistance, and they often cover a wide variety of problems and situations, including substance abuse and emotional and mental problems. Services can be scheduled free of charge. Reach out to your HR department to see if your company has an EAP to offer.

DRUG AND ALCOHOL SELF-ASSESSMENT

1. Do you drink or use to overcome shyness or to feel more confident?

2. Are you having money troubles because of drinking or using?

3. Do you ever stay home from work because of drinking or using?

4. Is drinking or using causing trouble in your family?

5. Is drinking or using giving you a bad reputation?

6. Have you lost a job or a business because of drinking or using?

7. Do you drink or use to escape your problems?

8. Do you drink or use when you are alone?

9. Do you have blackouts? (Loss of memory for events that happened or of actions you performed while drinking or using?)

10. Do you feel remorse after drinking or using?

11. Do you need a drink at a definite time every day?

12. Do you drink in the morning?

13. Have you ever been in a hospital because of drinking or using?

14. Has a doctor ever treated you for your drinking or using?

15. Do you drink or use too much at the wrong time?

16. Do you make promises to yourself or others about your drinking or using?

17. Do you have to keep on drinking or using once you have started?

18. Is drinking or using making it hard for you to sleep?

19. Have you had an accident because of drinking or using?

20. Do you drink or use to relieve the painfulness of living?

21. Do you have trouble disposing of cans or bottles?

22. Are you less particular about people you are with and the places you go when you are drinking or using?

23. Have you been arrested more than once for drunk driving or driving under the influence of drugs?

24. Has drinking or using affected your health?

If you have answered "Yes" to any of these questions, you may have an alcohol or drug problem.

Two or more yes answers indicate you have problems with alcohol and/or drugs and should seek help immediately.

ACKNOWLEDGEMENTS

I would like to express my gratitude to some extraordinary people I am blessed to have in my life. Without them I would not have written this book: matter of fact, without each and every one of them I doubt I'd even still be around to entertain the thought.

First, to my family: to my sister Kate, who refused to let me lie/bluff/squirm my way out of getting help. I really do think I agreed to go to treatment so you would lay off, but oh my ever-loving God, am I thankful you were so damn persistent. To my brother, who has always been such an incredible source of strength and comfort, especially after Dad had to go: George, you have helped me through some really lonely and dark times. I love you more than you know.

To my Dad: oh, I would give anything to have just one more day with him. He and I grew to really know each other on this whack-a-doo journey. We threw off all pretense and we got so real. His love and support were a gift the size of which I can't describe, and I am beyond thankful for each precious moment. I would love to share with him all I've learned, and how I've grown. He would get such a kick out of it.

To my AA home group, and the beautiful souls who became a second family to me. You accepted me unconditionally from the start, began teaching me what loving yourself looks like, showed me it was okay to be broken, and eventually taught me to see the beauty in the fissures. You showed me how to laugh at myself in a healthy and healing way, and oh, what a lifesaver that has been. To all, but in particular Bob, Pat, Bernie, Paul, Steve, and Ted, you each shared a bit of your serenity with me and made me hungry for more. Bob, you helped get me through the ugly, disconcerting reality I had been running from, and you did it absolutely selflessly. I will only be able to repay you by continuing to pay it forward (and by joining you on the occasional Bingo outing. You pro.)

Bruce and Joan, for the friendship you gave my folks, especially Dad, and for the friendship and love you've continued to give our little brood, I thank you. Bruce, you were like a brother to Dad, and you helped him really understand this horrible, gorgeous, mysterious disease called addiction. You've both shown me first-hand how important, how imperative it is to stay diligent. You and Joanie will always be as much a part of my heart as my own flesh and blood.

To my Ally girls: you took care of both me and my fuzzy kids at a time I was unable to do either. I am beyond thankful for this remarkable (Dad's word for them) group of women I am blessed to call my friends. Because of your kindness, love and unbelievable generosity, my pups received wonderful care, and I didn't have to worry about a thing except getting better. What a tremendous gift!

Jen, you know I would never have gone if you hadn't reassured me 8,042 times that my babies would be okay. And arranged for me to go to detox. And get my car home. And coordinate everything else. Diana, I can't imagine what a jolt it must have been for you to be thrust into the world of alcoholism so brutally (via my behavior and inability to even write my name), but you didn't miss a beat. You carted my happy ass to the detox center like we were going shoe shopping. If I remember correctly, we even laughed a couple of times. Kem, you were instrumental in helping coordinate "project Susan", and you have lifted my spirits in so many ways since I got sober. I've lost count of the unexpected texts, or the notes in the mail just letting me know *you* know some days are harder than others. You always seem to time it so perfectly: those sweet, loving gestures have chased away some incredibly dark clouds.

To Dave: you have been a mentor, a friend, a stalwart believer in who I owed it to myself and others to be. You didn't give up on me when I had given up on myself. You were kind when I needed support, tough when I needed accountability, and ever, ever diligent in letting me know through it all it was because you wanted me to be well.

To Britt and her Tim, who knew what I was before I knew, who cared with such diligence and tenderness for me and my kitties both during my rehab and so many times after, who have graced me with such unconditional love, support and encouragement: I am so blessed to have you in my life.

To Katie and my Tim, who each had the incredible courage and love for me to come visit during my time in treatment: you will never know what seeing your beautiful faces did for my spirits and my heart at what was without doubt the scariest time of my life. To do that was such a precious, selfless gift, and it helped me to continue putting one foot in front of the other. Oh, how I love you both.

To my Valley Hope counselors, caregivers and staff: I came into that treatment center more terrified than I have ever been in my entire life, both of what I was facing and what I was learning about myself. Throughout the check-in process, all I wanted to do was run. You believed in me before I could even consider that possibility. You created such a nurturing, safe and supportive environment that I quickly began to understand nothing was off-limits, and I began to realize how incredibly sick I really was. I began to understand how many people who had been as sick as I was weren't around anymore because of this devastating, often fatal disease of addiction. The combination of factors making up your program hit me from all angles, answering questions I didn't know I had, and giving me the platform on which I could begin to heal. You didn't force me out of my comfort zone. You yanked me out without so much as a "how do you do," but with each step you let me know I was in a safe place, and I could speak my truths without anyone judging me or hurting me.

To Author Academy Elite: Kary, Niccie, Nanette, Tina and the countless others who have been instrumental in helping make this little book a reality, thank you. The belief you had in me from the start has been a tremendous part of my growth as a person, as a writer and as an advocate for others who will see their stories reflected in mine. You have all been such a blessing, in so many ways. I can't wait to see what lies ahead!

To my H.P., aka the God of my understanding: how cool is it, how *amazing* is it how we've grown to know each other so well? (Okay. I know You've always known me. Work with me here.) I am in awe of You, and in awe of who You have created me to become. Let's keep on doing what we're doing. I am so in love with our relationship. You give me strength, the right words and such keen intuition each and every day, at just the right time. Thank you. Thank you.

To the tragic, beautiful, tender souls I've met at meetings, at detox centers, at rehabs and through the course of my daily life: thank you for trusting me to share your time and your stories. Know you are precious and you are worth saving. This world needs you in it. Sometimes it takes a while to fully understand that: that's how it was for me. The world *does* need you. My hope for each of you is someday you will decide to embrace this walk so you can fully understand how true that is. How important you are. How much your story is needed—and it's not completely written yet.

You will all forever have a place in my heart. You are the reason I am able to share what I've learned, and what I continue to learn each and every day. I love each one of you with every ounce of my being.

A gift? Hell, no. What each of you has given me are a thousand tiny miracles.

Susan Lynn
January 2020

DISCUSSION POINTS

1. What do you feel is the worst thing that could happen if you embark on a journey of recovery? What are you afraid might happen?

2. What is the best thing that could happen if you got sober?

3. Is there a single "biggest obstacle" holding you back from starting a new, sober life? What is it? What power does this obstacle hold?

4. How would the people in your inner circle react to your decision to begin recovery? Who would you tell? Who would support you, no matter what? Who might try to sabotage you?

5. What is your biggest motivator to get control of your life back? Why?

6. What are you waiting for?

ABOUT THE AUTHOR

Susan Lynn is a writer, speaker, podcaster and recovery advocate. She has spent the better part of the last five years joyfully sober, sharing what she's learned with other addicts and those who love them. Her greatest joy is working with others new to the recovery journey, taking her message to groups and individuals ready to truly start living. Connect with Susan at www.theoptimisticdrunk.com, *on Twitter at* The Optimistic Drunk@ DrunkOptimistic *and on Facebook at* The Optimistic Drunk@blessingsofaddiction.

Make sure to visit 'theoptimisticdrunk.com' and sign up on our e-mail list: you'll have access to a vast amount of relevant and valuable information.

- Get a "sneak-peek" at the newest releases in *The Optimistic Drunk* book series and podcasts.

- Listen to the latest podcasts and re-visit your favorites.

- Learn about online classes and courses.

- Attend a seminar or help organize one in your area.

- Participate in contests and giveaways.

- Explore easy tools to help you live your best sober life!

CPSIA information can be obtained
at www.ICGtesting.com
Printed in the USA
JSHW021114080320
4612JS00005B/12

9 781647 460983